CONTENTS

Introducing

OTTO FRANK

EDITH FRANK

MARGOT FRANK

ANNE FRANK

MR DUSSEL

MRS VAN DAAN

PETER VAN DAAN

MR VAN DAAN

The first one to welcome me was you, diary, probably the most beautiful of all my gifts.

Sunday, 14 June 1942.
On Friday, 12 June, I woke up at six in the morning, which was to be expected, since it was my birthday.

I always wanted to start writing in a diary...

... but, now, I ask myself, who could be interested in the secrets of a 13-year-old girl?

Anyway, I'll never show it to anyone. Unless, one day, I find a true friend – boy or girl – with whom to share my secrets.

Which is why I'm writing this diary.

Look, Moortje. I'd like to introduce you to my new diary, named Kitty.

Lately, my dad, whom I like to call Pim, has been staying home, since he's retired from business.

Pim...

If you're worried about some of my grades, I promise you, they'll get better soon.

That's not it, dear. Your grades are fine.

Listen, Anne, you might have noticed a few pieces of furniture are missing from our home. We've been moving them.

We want to be prepared, in case we have to hide.

But, Dad ... when will that happen?

Don't worry. Your mum and I will take care of everything. Just trust me.

11

Two shirts, three pairs of underwear, a dress, a skirt, a jacket, a summer coat, two pair of socks ... I was suffocating walking under all of that.

My father has made the Germans believe our family had fled to Switzerland through Belgium.

I believe it's a matter of time until we find out if that lie has worked.

Here we are.

13

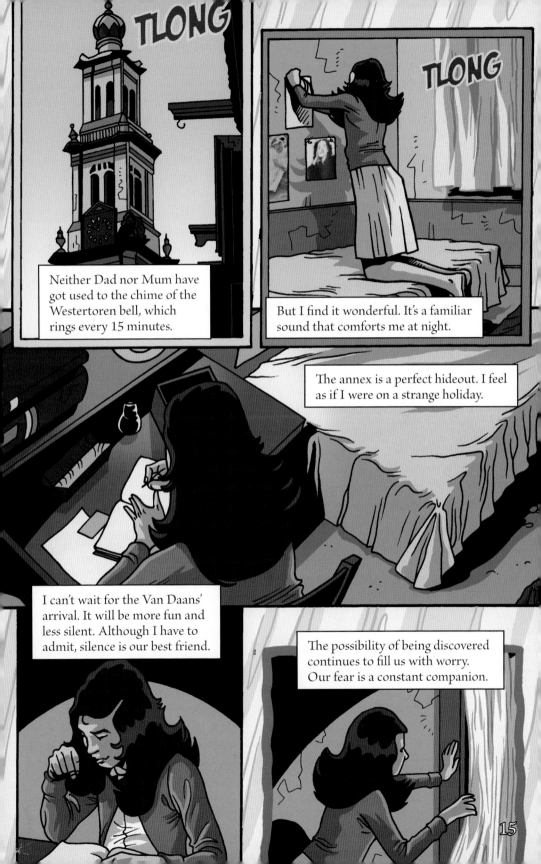

TLONG

TLONG

Neither Dad nor Mum have got used to the chime of the Westertoren bell, which rings every 15 minutes.

But I find it wonderful. It's a familiar sound that comforts me at night.

The annex is a perfect hideout. I feel as if I were on a strange holiday.

I can't wait for the Van Daans' arrival. It will be more fun and less silent. Although I have to admit, silence is our best friend.

The possibility of being discovered continues to fill us with worry. Our fear is a constant companion.

From the start of their arrival, we've eaten every meal together in a warm atmosphere.

Anne, go call your father. Dinner is almost ready.

The people covering for us are also the ones in charge of bringing us food.

But along with the Van Daans comes terrible news...

Beans, vegetables, peas ... we can't complain food-wise.

It's horrible. Things are harder and harder on the outside.

The Jewish-Dutch families are being deported by land or sea to the northern part of Holland to concentration camps. For the first time, we feel lucky to be alive, safe and sound.

17

19

The annex is awful, but it is still a thousand times better than the outside world.

Miep, one of the people covering for us, says all of our Jewish friends have been sent away on cattle trains to the Westerbork Camp.

Old people, kids, women ... the Gestapo doesn't forget anyone.

Of course Westerbork is just the first stop, the gateway to farther and more horrible camps. The BBC talks of gas chambers...

I feel sick just thinking about it.

21

Keep voices down at all times. Especially until 6.00 p.m. That's when the people in the office next door leave.

Exercise every day.

Rest between 10.00 p.m. and 8.00 a.m.

English, French, maths, writing and history lessons. At all times.

Breakfast: 9.00 a.m.
Lunch: 1.15 to 1.45 p.m.
Dinner: hot or cold, no fixed time.

Washing: Sundays starting at 9.00 a.m. in the kitchen, bathroom or private office. The rules aren't that hard!

23

The Nazis don't respect anyone. Not pregnant women, the elderly, the young or the sick. Everyone travels to death.

You can see plenty of orphans on the streets...

They've lost their families and friends to the Nazis. Dirty and underfed, they are simply trying to survive one more day.

Dussel's words make us all feel lucky. How good we have it here – sheltered and calm.

25

It's a real challenge to keep ourselves entertained: riddles, jokes, English and French practice, book reviews ... anything that helps interrupt the boredom.

So much so that we decided to celebrate both St Nicholas and Hanukkah holidays this year.

It was the first time any of us in the annex celebrated St Nicholas. It was a lot of fun!

A few days after, Mr Van Daan ordered a few pounds of meat to make sausages and cold cuts.

It was very weird to see our living room turn into a true butcher shop!

The battle goes on for hours, until finally, the silence comes back...

The next day, the city wakes up destroyed. We see the horror in broad daylight.

More than 200 dead, and many, many wounded, the radio announces.

Terrible destruction.

Dozens of kids searching for their parents among the still-hot debris...

... slightly hopeful that they would find them wounded, but still alive.

For us, when the fear of the bombs lifts, the fear of being discovered returns.

In the days that follow, several more bombings happen over Amsterdam.

The smoke and stench from the fire become normal, even in our shelter.

Which often tends to result in more arguments than usual.

CHAPTER 3
WORDS OF HOPE

Except when we listen to the BBC on the radio. The hope we have of hearing some good news causes a miracle – we all manage to be quiet.

All those hours listening to the radio pay off; we finally hear some great news...

Friday, 10 September 1943
Dear Kitty:
Every time I sit down to write, something special has happened,

Italy has surrendered without any conditions!

In doing so, Germany has lost one of its main allies. It's comforting news.

But, sadly, it hasn't improved the mood in the annex.

Living with you is punishment!

You're so selfish!

Crazy old woman!

You're as stubborn as a mule! It's just a stupid jacket! We need the money!

Never!

And it's even worse when they make up.

39

... looking for a way out that isn't there.

The dream is always the same. I'm alone, inside a prison...

But every time I manage to get outside, it's even worse. I lose my last hope.

And I wake up.

In fact, I turn red so easily now!

Luckily, the illness doesn't last long. In a few days, I get my colour back.

All the changes, visible and invisible, that my body is going through seem wonderfully confusing to me.

But so far I've only trusted you, Kitty, with my secrets.

So you'll understand if I need someone else to talk to.

Hi ... Sorry ... are you busy?

I like looking at his black-blue eyes and his half-smile.
And I can tell he is shy and self-conscious.

44

45

And the horror only gives way to everyday patterns.

Household chores.

Fear.

Hope.

Confinement.

I want to escape. But I've got nowhere to go. There's only one place where I find peace...

49

... and that's with Peter.

Hi.

Oh, uh ... hi, I was just chopping wood.

Yeah, I can tell. I'm not blind.

Ha, right. Sorry. How silly of me.

His shyness, which I used to find annoying, is now one of the things I like about him.

I know that, given time, I'll get him to open up his heart.

Aren't you scared? You could get hurt.

Scared? No ... I'm not scared of anything.

Not of anything?

No.

Spiders?

No.

Ghosts?

Ha ... no.

Bombs? Machine guns?

I've got used to all of that. Only one thing scares me, sometimes...

... my own thoughts.

I can't get away from them.

51

My personal worries took a step back due to an upsetting event.

Mr Van Daan was doing his nightly rounds in the front building. And a noise caught his attention.

Who's there?

There was nobody there. Or at least that's what Mr Van Daan thought when he saw the front door was locked.

But the next morning...

Things are missing! They took the projector, and the front door was wide open!

That could only mean one thing. That the thief had spent quite some time in the office. And he had a copy of the key.

Sorry ... am I bothering you?

I was wondering if I could come and write in my diary in here – with you. As you know, Mr Dussel is in my bedroom, working on his research ... and we can't stand each other anymore...

Of course you can.

Peter is the only one who keeps to himself and doesn't bother the others.

I'd love to know what Peter thinks about all this, about my thoughts, my wishes. If only I could talk to him.

Tell him how I feel about him, how I love him. But I can't. I can't!

If only he were a little less shy... Then he could get to know the real Anne. The Anne he doesn't know just yet. The real me.

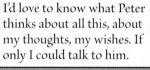

How can he come to love me if he only knows one side of me?

Oh, Peter ... if only I could talk to you.

55

Yesterday, a plane crashed nearby.

What an awful thing to do!

The Germans are a bunch of cowards.

Come on, don't let the outside war take your happiness away. We already have enough to deal with in here.

Come on, a little smile!

Why do you always want me to smile?

CHAPTER 4
ANNE, THE WRITER

The Germans killed the pilots as they flew by the crash.

Because your dimples come out when you smile. They're lovely.

Don't say that. I know I'm not beautiful. Never have been, never will be.

It was horrible. But there was nothing we could do.

We spent two days in total silence. We hardly slept at all and were sick with fear when, finally, we heard more footsteps...

CLOMP!
CLOMP!

The police!

But this time around, it was the people covering for us, Miep and Henk.

Easy, it's over now.

We all shed tears of joy when we realized it was them. They told us that it was the security guard who had alerted the police.

It's a miracle you didn't get caught! But please, don't ever leave the annex again. It's too dangerous for you to go down to the offices!

You are here in secret! You put us all in danger by exposing yourselves that way.

Mr Henk is right. We are Jews. At this time, we don't have rights, only duties.

65

As the days go by, the strain between my father and me reaches a tipping point. So, I decide to write him a letter and tell him how I feel.

I put all of my frustration into it, all the feelings I've kept inside during my time in the annex.

The pain...

The fear...

RATATATAT

BOOM!

The relationship with my mother that can't be fixed.

And throughout all of it, this is the only comfort I've found.

I hope Pim understands. He's the only adult I still trust in this house.

67

The rest of them are being mean, as usual.

You've been in there for half an hour, Mr Dussel! You're not the only one living in this house.

Silence, please, Mr Van Daan!

Now I'm to blame?

You have no right to tell my husband to shut up!

Do it yourself, then!

But then, a piece of news interrupts the fighting.

LOOK AT THIS!

INVASION!

No one can believe it, but it finally happened.

But we still have a long way to go. It could be a year until the war is finally over. And its outcome is still uncertain.

The joy in the annex quickly vanishes when we find out that our grocer has been arrested for hiding Jews.

Now we'll have to ration our food even more.

I've just turned 15. But I feel that I'm much older and that I know myself much better.

I know now I am many different things.

Everyone knows Anne the joker, the shallow girl, the confident girl.

But there's another part of me only you know, Kitty.

A more emotional, sensitive Anne.

And hiding this other part of me is exhausting.

I'm still trying to become a better version of myself and maybe someday I will be...

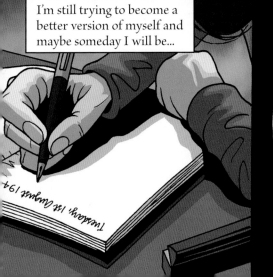

... if it weren't for all the other people in the world.

71

ANNE FRANK'S STORY: A LEGACY

When Adolf Hitler, leader of the National Socialist Workers' Party, or the Nazi's, became leader of Germany in 1933, the Frank family could imagine that difficult times would come. This totalitarian party was anti-Semitic, which means it hated Jews. That caused a drastic change in the life of all German Jews.

Among other things, the government increasingly restricted the daily lives of Jews, such as assigning specific places for transit or recreation, separate from the rest of the Germans. Jews soon became victims of the Holocaust, the systematic persecution and extermination plan carried out in different concentration camps. This situation continued and worsened during World War II (1939–1945). During the war, Germany occupied several countries, among them Poland and Holland. There, the Nazis captured all Jews. This included the Frank family and their companions, the Van Pels and Mr Pfeffer (who appear in Anne's diary as the Van Daans and Mr Dussel). They were discovered in August 1944, after two years of hiding.

In 1945, after the Soviets liberated Auschwitz, one of the cruellest concentration camps, Otto Frank returned to Amsterdam. He soon learned of the death of his entire family. Later, Miep Gies, one of the Franks' loyal protectors while they were in hiding, gave him Anne's diary. It was the only thing left in the house after the arrest. Two years later, Otto fulfilled Anne's wishes and published her diary. It was titled *The Secret Annex*, just as Anne had wished.

After the diary's publication, Otto received and answered many letters from Anne's readers. This work, and his ongoing fight for human rights around the world, continued until his death. The diary became a testament to the victims of the Holocaust and was translated into 67 languages.

"The back house", or "the annex", was transformed into a museum thanks to Otto's efforts to preserve and restore it. In 1960, it opened to the public under the name the "Anne Frank House". Today, almost one million people visit it every year. Those who visit can tour the rooms and take part in different activities and workshops. These activities are designed to promote respect for human rights and warn about the dangers of anti-Semitism, racism and discrimination. In 2010, on the museum's 50th anniversary, Anne's writings were exhibited to the public.

ABOUT ANNE FRANK

Anne Frank was born in 1929 in Frankfurt, Germany. She lived with her parents, Otto and Edith, and her older sister, Margot. With Hitler's rise to power in 1933, they had to leave for Amsterdam. After the beginning of World War II, Germany invaded Holland, and the Frank family found itself in danger again. They decided to hide in a secret house behind Otto Frank's office. That same year, Anne received a diary as a birthday gift, a diary she would fill with her experiences and thoughts. In 1944, the residents of the hideout were betrayed by some of their Dutch neighbours and the Gestapo arrested them. They were deported from Holland, and both Anne and her sister were sent to the Bergen-Belsen concentration camp. In March 1945, shortly before the camp was liberated and the war was over, they both died of typhus fever. Otto Frank was the only surviving family member.

ANNE FRANK AND FILM

In 1959, *The Diary of Anne Frank* made its debut. It was a film based on a theatre play of the same name. Even though the film wasn't a box office hit, it received three Academy Awards, or Oscars. It was one of the first Hollywood films to tackle the persecution of Jews. Since then, the Holocaust has been featured in more than 20 feature films and documentaries.

Schindler's List was directed by Steven Spielberg in 1993. It was based on the novel *Schindler's Ark*, by Thomas Keneally. It tells the story of Oskar Schindler, a German businessman who sheltered 1,000 Jews in his factory, saving them from the Holocaust. This film received multiple awards, including seven Oscars.

Life Is Beautiful is a famous 1997 Italian film set in 1939. It tells the tender yet sad story of the imaginary games that Guido, a Jewish Italian man, makes up so that his son, Giosué, can handle, and finally survive, life in a concentration camp. This film is based on a book written by an Auschwitz survivor.

In 2002, Roman Polanski brought *The Pianist* to the big screen. It tells the story of Wladyslaw Szpilman, a Polish pianist and composer who survived both the Warsaw ghetto and World War II. His memoir, *The Pianist: The Extraordinary Story of One Man's Survival in Warsaw, 1939–45*, is one of many horrible tales depicting the Holocaust. In it, Szpilman recounts his life and how he escapes death after a German officer discovered him. The officer asked him to play a Chopin piece in exchange for letting him live. The film received many awards, including three Oscars.

GLOSSARY

Allied forces countries united against Germany during World War II, including Great Britain, France, the United States, Canada, and others

annex extra building that is joined onto or placed near a main building

arrogant exaggerating one's own self-worth or importance, often in an overbearing manner

atmosphere mood or feeling of a place

BBC British Broadcasting Corporation; a British public service broadcaster that produces radio and TV shows

chamber pot type of bowl that people used as a toilet

concentration camp place where thousands of people are held under harsh conditions

confrontational acting in a threatening way, usually to argue with someone else

defend try to keep someone or something from being harmed

deport send people back to their own country

extermination killing or destroying someone or something

gas chamber room where people are killed with poison gas

Gestapo secret police of Nazi Germany; the Gestapo is a subdivision of the SS

ghetto run-down, enclosed part of a city; where Jews were forced to live during World War II

interrupt get in the way of someone

loyal being true to something or someone

Nazi member of a political party led by Adolf Hitler; the Nazis ruled Germany from 1933 to 1945

orphan child whose parents have died

persecution cruel or unfair treatment, often because of race or religious beliefs

ration limit to prevent running out of something

retired person who has given up work usually because of his or her age

socialize get together or talk with other people in a friendly way

support help and encourage someone

tolerant able to put up with something

totalitarian of or relating to a political system in which the government has complete control over the people

DISCUSSION QUESTIONS

1. Why do you think Anne Frank's story has touched so many readers?

2. Mrs Van Daan thinks Anne is a spoilt child. Do you agree? Explain your answer.

3. Do you think you could live a long time locked inside your home? Why or why not?

WRITING PROMPTS

1. Anne Frank described most of her everyday life while she was locked up in the secret annex. What do you think a day in your life would be like if you were locked in your home? What would you do and what wouldn't you do? Write a letter to a friend describing your experience.

2. Anne received her diary when she was 13, which helped her realize that she wanted to be a writer. Write a paragraph describing one of your favourite gifts. What makes it so special?

3. Imagine if the Frank family hadn't been arrested and instead was able to leave their hideout in peace. Pretend you're Anne. Write a diary entry about the first thing you would have done once you left the annex.

ABOUT THE AUTHOR

Diego Agrimbau, from Buenos Aires, Argentina, has written more than a dozen graphic novels for various publishing houses around the world. He has won multiple awards, among them the 2005 Prix Utopiales for *Bertold's Bubble*, the 2009 Premio Planeta DeAgostini for Comic Books for *Planet Extra* and the 2011 Premio Dibujando entre Culturas for *The Desert Robots*. He's currently a contributor to *Fierro* magazine and writes "Los Canillitas" comic scripts for the newspaper *Tiempo Argentino*.

ABOUT THE ILLUSTRATOR

Fabián Mezquita, from Argentina, started publishing his work in 1998. In 2001, he worked for a year as an assistant, and then continued his career as an illustrator, working for ad agencies and various publishing houses, both in Argentina and abroad. He is a founding and active member of Banda Dibujada, a cultural organization created to promote comic books for children and young adults.

FIND OUT MORE
BOOKS

Anne Frank: Biography, Ann Kramer (QED Publishing, 2014)

Remember World War II: Kids Who Survived Tell Their Stories, Dorinda Nicholson (National Geographic Society, 2015)

The Diary of a Young Girl, Anne Frank (Puffin, 2015)

WEBSITES

www.bbc.co.uk/schools/primaryhistory/world_war2/world_at_war/
Learn more about World War II and the Holocaust at this BBC website.

www.theholocaustexplained.org/
Find out more about the Holocaust at this website from the London Jewish Cultural Centre.

INDEX